Sally –
The Unhomeable
Greyhound

Lorraine Bullman

Table of Contents

Acknowledgements

With thanks to my parents, who have supported me in everything I've done. You're both amazing.

To my husband John, for his support throughout all my greyhound fundraising and awareness endeavours.

To Ann, who introduced me to greyhounds and had faith long before we did that John and I would give Sally a home. Hope you and Sally are looking after each other up there, over the bridge.

Thank you to my good friend Hilary who donated her time to assist with editing the book and without whom Sally's story might never have been published.

Thank you to everyone who works in greyhound welfare, whether by raising awareness of what great pets they are or by looking after them in homing kennels.

Lastly, thank you to the greyhounds, especially Sally and Sky: you are my inspiration in all the volunteer work I do.

A minimum of 25% from the sale of this book will be going to help various greyhound charities.

Thinking of adopting a greyhound, or maybe a sighthound? Please do contact your local rescue centre. Greyhounds are surprisingly versatile and can adapt to many different lifestyles. Meet a greyhound and I defy you not to fall in love!

List of useful websites for more information:

Greyhound Trust
www.greyhoundtrust.org.uk/

Forever Hounds Trust
www.foreverhoundstrust.org/

Greyhound Gap
www.greyhoundgap.org.uk/

Fen Bank Greyhound Sanctuary
www.fenbankgreyhounds.co.uk/

Norfolk Greyhound Rescue
www.norfolkgreyhoundrescue.co.uk/

Greyhound Walks
www.greyhoundwalks.co.uk/

Great Global Greyhound Walk
www.greatglobalgreyhoundwalk.co.uk/

Discovering greyhounds

I have always liked animals, and since being given a book about horses as a child, they were my first love. I grew up buying magazines and books, and having pony rides on the beach whenever opportunities arose. Eventually I had riding lessons and then when I passed my driving test I realised that the horse-racing headquarters of the UK (if not the world) was within an hour's drive of where I lived. Newmarket was heaven to me, horses everywhere, and I watched them on the gallops, at the races and attended stud tours.

We had dogs at home. My early years were spent with Rusty, a golden labrador, and when he passed on, we had Rex. I was scared of him! He was a collie cross. Long-legged and fast, maybe he had some greyhound in him. I was young and he was a puppy with sharp teeth. He was a gorgeous dog to look at, but he had little manners. When we moved home it was decided that Rex would be better suited to someone who had the knowledge and time to train him, and so we became a dogless family when I was only seven years old. And so it was for the rest of my growing-up.

My school years were filled with weekly riding lessons, along with occasional gymkhana and 'own a pony' days. When I left education and I was working and earning money, I wanted to support charities that looked after racehorses when their careers had finished so I donated money when possible and visited the charities to see the horses I was helping, albeit in a small way.

One day I began to think that greyhounds had a similar fate to racehorses, over-bred for the racing industry and not always cared for after their careers were over. I don't remember it being any one particular thing that made me think about greyhounds. We had been greyhound racing a couple of times in the past, or we might have seen it on TV; whatever the reason, I think it was fate that brought greyhounds into our lives. Deciding I'd like to help these dogs, I searched the internet and found a local branch of the Retired Greyhound Trust (now the Greyhound Trust) that ran a sponsorship scheme

I got in touch and sponsored a handsome brindle greyhound who had epilepsy. After asking if I could meet him, I went to have my first-ever meeting with a greyhound. Austin was a very gentle soul, which I'd later discover to be the normal characteristic of a retired greyhound. He let me stroke him and I asked the lady who ran the kennels lots of questions. Then we took him into the enclosed paddock – wow, did he run fast! I was astonished. With his long legs, he flew round in circles. His epilepsy was under control and Austin got his chance a couple of months later to go to his forever home, where he had some hound friends to live with and a sofa to lie on. I continued to visit the homing kennels every month or so, to take donated goods and spend some time with the hounds. With Austin in his new home, I had to choose another hound to sponsor.

Sally had not been in the kennels long. She had been homed straight from racing kennels to a couple who already had a greyhound, but after two years with them they had to move to accommodation that allowed only one dog. Sally was last one in and first one out, but maybe her tendencies to be nervous and chew and destroy things were the real reasons they decided to let her go.

In the homing kennels Sally settled into the routine, but it must have been strange and very unsettling for her after those years in a home. When I met her for the first time, she had to be held tightly or she would have fled back into her kennel. Her eyes were wide open, a bit scared and bewildered, but I sat quietly with her, stroking her, and she relaxed.

Sally when I first met her, wide eyed and scared

Unusually for greyhounds, Sally was a barker... and her bark was loud! She barked in the kennels

6

whenever visitors came to look at the dogs; anything new or unusual would set her off. It was near impossible to talk over the top of her.

After the initial meeting, whenever visiting the kennels, I always asked to spend a little time with Sally, and slowly she barked less when I arrived and settled quicker with me. Never having walked a dog in my life, I plucked up the courage to ask whether I could take her for a walk. I needn't have been so worried; Sally was a dream and looked after me! She walked so nicely beside me and I was beginning to get attached to her. A while later I asked if I could take her home for the day. I had no intention of giving her a home – I'd never been responsible for any pet throughout the 30 plus years of my life and having a dog was not something I had given any thought to. However, I thought it would be good for Sally to get out of the kennels for a day and I would enjoy it too. We certainly had a lovely time. We walked into town, saw my parents, and then headed home for Sally to eat her dinner, which she ate up – a sign that she was relatively relaxed. Then we chilled out in front of the TV. Sally decided she'd rather stay in the hallway, but I sat in the room on the floor and after a while she came to join me. Such a small gesture, but it meant so much!

As you can imagine, this beautiful fawn and white hound was beginning to get under my skin. My husband John first met her when she was taken for a day out of the kennels to a local fun dog show. When walking her round the showground we noticed that she didn't like standing about, preferring to walk and keep on the move. So, John (also an animal lover, but like me with no experience of looking after any pet) and I had discussions and asked if we could have Sally to stay for a night. By this time, Sally, despite her beautiful looks, had acquired quite a reputation as being unhomeable, mainly due to the constant loud barking whenever anyone came to visit the kennels. She just put everyone off. Friends later said they remember visiting the kennels at that time and Sally would be barking her head off.

Sally came to stay for a Saturday night and was very calm and quiet. There was some panting early on, but she was then relatively settled. Overnight we heard her moving about. and not being used to sharing our home with an animal we got little sleep! The weekend led to more serious discussions as to whether we could give Sally a home. It was decided we'd have her for a long weekend over Easter. Once again that weekend Sally behaved so well. The only question was whether we wanted to commit to an animal in our lives. I suffered from depression and was wary, unsure if having Sally would help or increase my stress levels. By this time Sally was nine years old, still full of life, but her age would have been another reason for her being unlikely to find a home easily. In our eyes, though, it would be less of a commitment in terms of years than a much younger dog. I think Sally had already decided that she was happy with us and wanted to live with us, and she'd tried her best to tell us in her own way by behaving so well with us amateur dog-sitters. At the end of the weekend we took her back to the kennels and she instantly started barking – she did not want to go back there, and we didn't want her to. We had a fortnight's holiday to Scotland booked the following month and arranged that we would give Sally her forever home when we returned.

The next time I visited the kennels to see Sally before our holiday, she came flying out of her kennel to see me and leapt up at me, giving me a big hug. I was in tears! How could there ever have been any doubt that we would give her a home? We went on holiday and sent her a postcard saying we'd soon be home to pick her up.

As we needed a home check, the kennel owner brought Sally to us and I remember when she left that I suddenly thought, Oh my! This living, breathing animal is here to stay and is our responsibility! I needn't have worried, Sally looked after us and taught us all about looking after a greyhound. I took the first week off work and worked on leaving Sally home alone, little by little building up the time she was left by herself. She'd been known to have issues with separation anxiety in her previous home so we knew this could be a challenge. Again, Sally showed her desire to live with us, and except for one destroyed cushion, showed no signs of distress.

One of the first photos of Sally in our garden

The first few months

During the first few weeks Sally showed us how much she loved walkies. She would have gone out every hour, on the hour, if she could. It made us realise how frustrated she must have been in the kennels. No wonder she barked so much; she wanted to get out of there! She certainly had every care possible in those homing kennels, and so much love, too, but we soon found out how much she liked to be out and about. She loved exploring our home area and got excited when she saw the local cats and wild rabbits. Within a week of homing Sally, we were walking not far from home when she spotted some rabbits and reared up, falling over backwards. It took us by surprise and our hearts were in our mouths, but she got up absolutely fine. However, it had taught us a lesson to keep her on a short lead, and to try and spot any wildlife before she did. Even in her later years, she still caught us out by jumping into someone's garden where a cat was hiding in a bush. We had her on a short lead and soon pulled her away safely, but there was no denying her prey instincts even in her twilight years.

We were lucky to have a small wood nearby which we could walk to, and when we first walked Sally there I thought it would be fun to see if she liked jumping over the fallen logs. My love of all things horsey took over and I jogged up to a fallen tree and jumped over, but it was many years since I'd played gymkhanas and I tripped and fell in a heap the other side! Sally in the meantime had joyfully jumped the log with ease, and with her lead still in my hand, I looked up to see her staring down at me as if to say, 'Whatever are you doing down there, Mum?' That was the start and end of our very short-lived game of jumping logs!

Sally didn't much enjoy car travel, but we carried on regardless and took her everywhere with us. She always settled better on the way home. Outings included the beach, where she was not over-keen on the water, but would paddle her paws on the shoreline on a warm day. The forest seemed to be her favourite habitat and she would happily sniff about and wander along.

Sally sunbathing, resting on a plank of wood!

We soon learned that most greyhounds love to sunbathe. Sally also enjoyed digging, so it became a fun time for her to dig a hole in the soil and then lie in it, lapping up the warmth of the sun. When she dug in inappropriate parts of the garden I decided to lay an odd flowerpot and plank of wood that we had spare in that

11

area to try to dissuade her. It didn't work – she still dug there and then she'd lie down with her head resting on the plank! It was fun to see her cheeky nature come out the more she settled into her new life. In fact, we continued to notice changes for up to 18 months after she came to live with us.

Sally roaching

When relaxed and happy, greyhounds lie on their backs with their feet in their air – it's called roaching, like a dead cockroach, and is the ultimate sign that a hound is settled. John and I had never seen a roaching hound before so it was quite a surprise and novelty to find Sally upside-down on her bed one evening. It had taken a couple of months, but she was obviously really beginning to feel at home. It was always going to take her a while, as she was a nervous type of dog, but with our naïve inexperienced way of looking after her, involving her in everything we did, she flourished. It was a mutual thing; we loved having Sally in our lives and she really enhanced our everyday life. We asked ourselves often how could there ever have been any doubt that giving Sally a home was going to work.

Our traditional Christmas is to have a party with my side of the family on Christmas Day evening. It can often last into the early hours of Boxing Day. With a little trepidation, we planned to carry on as normal and see how Sally got on, always with the option of leaving early if she didn't like it. We needn't have worried. Sally watched intently whilst we sat with our buffet tea on our laps, eyeing up each person to a get a titbit. Then when the fun and games started she lay down and watched us, not worried at all by the music and laughter.

Sally at Christmas

Holidays

Just over a year after giving Sally her forever home we thought we would try taking her on holiday. We knew she loved going to new places, but car travel was still a bit of an issue. It would be make or break to spend a whole week constantly getting in and out of the car. Thankfully it pretty much cured the problem and she did seem to travel better after that.

We chose the North York Moors as our destination and found a dog-friendly bungalow to rent for the week. On arriving, we unloaded the car and then let Sally off lead to explore the inside of the bungalow. She had a sniff round and soon lay down to rest after the long drive. When it came to bedtime, I fussed about trying to decide where best to put her bed, and in the end Sally decided for me. The bed had been dumped in the living room while we unpacked the car and she just took herself off to lie on it where it was. Problem sorted!

We had days out and about exploring the moors and villages. Sally was welcomed in the pubs we frequented and we all settled into holidaying together. One day was forecast to be wet and we decided to head to the preserved railway that went across the moors as there would be shelter and something to look at. Once we got there we began to wonder whether we might take Sally on her first train ride. There was a railway walk of about three miles. You could take the train to the next station, just a ten-minute ride, and then walk back. It sounded perfect for a first-time trip, so we bought our tickets – Sally had one too! The train was hauled by a large noisy steam engine, so we found a carriage at the back, away from the loco, and Sally jumped on board. She stood up all the way, just twitching her head and ears when the bogies banged as they went across the track. The short journey had gone well and we had a lovely walk to take us back to where we'd parked the car. We didn't realise at the time how much that train ride would shape the future. Not only had Sally proven that she was relatively happy to ride on a train, but it also reignited John's passion for trains. Visits to preserved railways was soon to be a hobby that would occupy a lot of our spare time.

Sally on her first train ride

As the first holiday had gone so well, we then booked up to go to Derbyshire later in the year. This gave Sally her first chance to do a bit of hill walking, ascending Mam Tor easily and enjoying the sights from the top of the peak. It was rather cold and breezy on the top, so we didn't stay long and headed to the Monsal Trail for a wander... we ended up wandering four miles, and as it was a linear walk, we had to do another four miles to get back to the car. Ten-year-old Sally was a trooper and carried on walking regardless, although she quickly jumped back into the car before we could decide to walk her any further! On visiting Chatsworth later in the week, we were asked by a Chinese lady whether she could take a photo of Sally. She certainly did look regal and very much at home, with the stunning grand house in the background. Indeed it is said that centuries ago greyhounds were only allowed to be owned by royalty.

Sally on the top of Mam Tor, Derbyshire

Yorkshire became our favourite holiday destination, and with its railway, history and dramatic wild landscape, the area around Ribblehead, part of the Settle-Carlisle Railway line, was often our chosen place to visit and walk. Sally loved the walking and exploring as much we did.

Sally in the grounds of Chatsworth House

We liked to find dog-friendly bed and breakfast accommodation and we stayed in some lovely ones, though the first one we tried didn't quite go to plan. The rooms were upstairs and as we lived in a bungalow we were unsure of how Sally would cope with stairs, but she hadn't had a problem when we encountered steps outside so hoped for the best. She managed to get up the stairs the first night, but was reluctant to come down in the morning. A lot of greyhounds have difficulty coming down stairs and will freeze at the top. With their long legs, it can take a bit of mastering to become accomplished at stairs when you're a hound. In the end, John had to carry Sally up and down the stairs for the rest of the week. Whether it was already planned or whether we gave them the idea, who knows, but this particular B&B did create a room downstairs which we were able to use the following year. We made a mental note to avoid places with upstairs in future.

We had a misunderstanding with one bed and breakfast, having thought that Sally would be able to join us in the breakfast room, but the owners were against this as they had other guests staying and didn't want to upset them. The first morning we took Sally for a walk round the village and then popped her in the car whilst we went in for breakfast. We came out to find an upset Sally and that the rear seat headrest covers had been chewed. We are not sure if separation anxiety had set in or if a cat had walked past (we'd seen several cats on our walk) but it was not an option to leave her in the car any more. Thankfully, when we chatted to the other guests at breakfast, they were very nice and had no problem with Sally being in the breakfast room, so with the owners' approval, Sally then joined us for breakfast each morning and we were all happy!

Sally relaxed, happy and roaching in a B&B room

On that same holiday, Sally gained a bit of attention when in the village pub she bagged the best place by lying down in front of the roaring log fire. We tried to move her as she was something of a trip hazard, but she was far too comfy and warm to move. The other customers were amused by her, not annoyed, so we left her to enjoy it.

On one visit to the Yorkshire Moors, we had a trip to the beach at Sandsend. It's a lovely expanse of beach and we walked Sally along the shoreline. She was enjoying herself, so I had the idea to see if she wanted to play in the water. We edged further into the sea, and in order to take a nice photo of us paddling, John encouraged us even further in. Seconds later a big wave headed towards us and I got drenched up to my knees. Sally cleverly jumped the wave and looked pretty pleased with herself. Did John capture the moment on film? Oh yes! I'm glad we gained something out of me having to sit in soaking wet jeans for the rest of the day!

The moment I got soaked, and Sally jumped over the wave at Sandsend

Trains

After her first experience of a train ride during our first holiday with her in Yorkshire, Sally came with us on many trips to various preserved railways up and down the country. She helped us make new friends as other people also took their dogs on the trains and we made great friendships through our pets and interest in railways. Sometimes Sally wouldn't settle so well on the journeys, but when a four-legged friend came along it really helped. Other times Sally was so relaxed that she would even roach on the train. The sight of her upside-down on the bench seat, on her blanket, made many people smile.

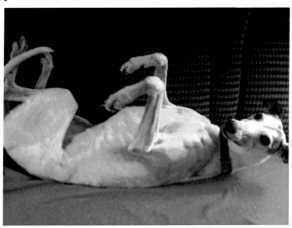

The first time Sally roached on a train

John preferred diesel engines to steam, so we usually attended when the diesel locos were running. Sally was still unsure of the hissing steam engines, but didn't bat an eyelid at the noisy-running diesels. In fact, she went to sleep once when we were sitting in the carriage behind a particular noisy diesel engine one day.

John and Sally with a heritage diesel loco

We would sometimes take a picnic on the train and one time I was eating some chicken and Sally was, of course, very interested. John then opened his spicy chicken tikka and instantly Sally ignored the plain chicken and went to plead for some of his meal. She loved spicy food, but we were careful to give her only very small nibbles which never upset her stomach.

Sally enjoying the train rides

Life with a greyhound

Sally showed us all about living with a greyhound and how they differ from other dogs.

If you have a greyhound, you soon find yourself carrying a blanket with you on your travels. Their bony frames can make it quite uncomfortable to lie on hard surfaces, so if you wanted your greyhound to relax and rest then you had to supply them with some comfort. We would regularly turn up at pubs with blanket in tow and people would look and think what a pampered dog with its own blanket! One of our favourite pubs took dog-friendliness to an extreme – as you entered there was a sign saying; dogs welcome, humans tolerated, and children on a lead! We would meet there for a walk around the village with our friends and their hounds and then head into the pub for lunch. There would sometimes be six hounds or more and we'd all have their blankets rolled up under our arms as we walked in. The floor was a sea of hounds when they'd all settled down! Greyhounds can curl up, but they also like to lie flat out, especially in entrances and hallways. I think that is down to the fact that they don't like to miss out on anything and it gives them the best chance of attracting a person for a stroke or treat.

A saying I have often heard is, 'Home a greyhound, lose a sofa!' Most greyhounds soon find how comfy sofas are and once they have tried one out, they are rarely found lying anywhere else. We didn't

Sally and her friends resting in the pub beer garden, complete with their own duvets to rest on!

encourage or discourage Sally from getting on the sofa and it took her over a year to try it. From that point I kept a throw on our two-seater sofa to protect it from dog hairs and dirty paws. Eventually Sally decided she really wanted to try our three-seater sofa, so she waited until I was at work and John was home alone with her, then jumped on it. John didn't mind, and with a smile at her cheekiness, he let her stay there. As soon as I came home Sally jumped off. She knew I didn't allow her on the larger sofa, mainly because of it not having a throw on it, but it looked like I would have to put a throw on both sofas as she found out she could stretch out even more on the large one!

Sally could be a bit finicky with food. On the whole she ate well, but sometimes would leave half of her tea. If we gave her anything new she'd give it a good smell and look at me as if to say, 'Are you sure its edible? Are you trying to poison me?' She didn't like biscuits very much and preferred soft treats. It was always hard getting pills down her as she became increasingly suspicious about what I was hiding in her food. This problem escalated when she needed more pills as she got older. I never did master the art of putting pills straight down her throat.

Having a greyhound brought us a large social life. After getting Sally our circle of friends grew immensely. Just by doing our daily walk, it could feel as if we were on a 'meet and greet' event, raising awareness of greyhounds as lovely pets, as most people had a comment to make. Greyhounds are a very noticeable breed, with their sleek lines and racing image, so the majority of passers-by recognised them. We soon got used to chatting to people about her and Sally was usually happy to let people stroke her, but she was wary of burly men. The best people to bump into were, of course, other sighthound owners. Greyhounds usually love to meet dogs of their own type and we humans could share endless stories about our special dogs.

We took Sally to local charity fun dog shows, and there were special greyhound shows, too, usually organised by the Greyhound Trust and their branches. She loved these events and on arrival in the car park would be whining with excitement when she saw all the other greyhounds.

Her greatest triumph in the show ring was at the annual Greyhound Extravaganza. We entered her in the Veteran Bitch class and she was nervous in the ring, but let the judge look at her. He was impressed with her condition for her age and placed her first! We were so proud of our girl. She rested up for a while and then had to return to the ring for the judging of Best in Show, but by this time she was tired and had had enough. She barked at the judge and wouldn't stop! We laughed and apologised.

The following year, Sally was still in great condition and we entered her again. This time she was placed second, which was ideal – she didn't have to wait around for the Best in Show judging and could go home before she got too tired.

When Sally won the Veteran Bitch class at the Greyhound Extravaganza

A few months after homing Sally we heard about the Greyhound Walks charity that held regular socialising walks around the East Anglia area. There was one locally in the forest and we took her along. She loved walking at the front of the pack and we enjoyed chatting with the other owners. We went along to most of the monthly walks and our circle of friends grew even more. There were often 50 hounds or more joining the walks, an impressive sight, but the amazing thing was the peace. There was an odd hound who liked to have a bark, but on the whole there was never any trouble or disagreements amongst the dogs.

The annual big walk was the Great Global Greyhound Walk (GGGW) and seeing how Sally enjoyed the walks, I was inspired to organise my own walk as part of this event. I was amazed when we had 52 hounds taking part. The next year we had nearly 100! I felt it was a very special event as it raised people's awareness across the world of greyhounds and their sighthound cousins as great pets. I went on to get more involved and join the team that runs the GGGW. I put this all down to Sally. Without her, I would never have become involved in the greyhound world as I have done and I wouldn't have so many special friendships.

Sally promoting the Great British Greyhound Walk, the forerunner to the GGGW. Helping me lead the walk and publicity photos wearing her GBGW bandana and Union Jack collar.

27

I also started to help run other fundraising events, and Sally was always there beside me, my inspiration. My wish is for all greyhounds to find a loving home and have the chance of a second life, just like Sally did with us, and by fundraising for homing charities and raising awareness I hope I will help with this.

Indeed, Sally can be credited with getting at least one ex-racing hound into a loving home, although indirectly she has probably helped several. We had to pop into the nearby city to renew John's photo driving licence, which at the time was only possible via the larger post offices. We took Sally along for the ride and combined it with a walk round the city park. As we walked back to the car at the shopping centre a lady asked if she could say hello to our dog. Sally was obliging and enjoyed the attention. The lady asked several questions, telling us that she was an assistant for a deaf and blind man who had recently lost his dog and wanted another one. We gave her the details of the kennels that Sally had come from and were delighted to find out a few weeks later that the gentleman had taken a greyhound into his home! We were able to keep in touch and it all worked out really well. Another human adopted by a greyhound!

For a few years we held events at the local horse charity where there was a large enclosed indoor arena that we hired. We could run the greyhounds off lead and most of them loved it. With their prey drive and speed, there are few opportunities for owners to allow their hounds off lead, so most people jumped at the chance to let their hounds have a run. Sally was a regular at the arena and was very sensible in her older years. If she felt good she would have a run, and if she felt a little stiff she would just have a sniff and trot about. One day we popped into the arena on our own to prepare for one of the event days. It was a warm day and Sally was 12 years old. As John and I had a look round and sorted out a few things, we let Sally off lead for a mooch about, but she didn't want a mooch, she wanted to RUN! She took off and ran round the arena. We watched nervously, but she was having a lovely time and as always looked after herself and soon stopped and rested.

Sally running in the horse arena

At the actual event a couple of weeks later, we were in two minds whether or not to take Sally with us. I was organising the event and needed to be at the arena all day. Sally's legs were beginning to show signs of weakness and she hadn't coped so well with the heat of the summer as in previous years, but knowing how much she liked to be with us we took her along, complete with comfy bed so she could lie down and rest as much as she liked. There was a space free in one of the off-lead sessions and after the other hounds had let off steam we decided to let Sally have a wander. When we took the lead off, she walked away and then suddenly took off across the arena at full stretch! Once again, she showed how she loved to run for fun, and liked to surprise us.

During a Greyhound Fun Day event at the arena there was a sausage race which was very popular with the hounds. This involved a row of three plates equally spread out with a bite-size piece of sausage on each. The hound had to race to the first plate, eat the sausage, and run to the second and eat that, and so on. Sally had entered a few of these and was pretty good, but on this particular day she was getting tired and as the other hounds lined up at the start, she lay down. No amount of persuading would get her up so the race began without her. She then decided that she'd better go and find those sausages and along the way she picked her way around the plates where other hounds had missed theirs. She had quite a feast and made us all laugh!

Sally having off-lead fun at a Greyhound Fun Day and then watching the other competitors in the sausage race and refusing to start!

We attempted to take Sally to horse trials to watch, but soon found out that it wound her up too much. We never knew if she wanted to run with the horses or chase them as they galloped past, but after we had tried twice for safety's sake we admitted defeat. She was fine with horses except for when they galloped; it really did fire her up.

With their calm natures greyhounds seem to win over even the most non-doggy people. Though I was an animal lover, I wasn't particularly a dog lover, but Austin and his friends soon won my heart, and showed me what beautiful animals they are – inside and out. Sally went on to work her charms on various friends and family when she came to live with us. Although we'd had dogs at home when I was young, my mum was not that keen on them; however, after she had met Sally a few times, she really began to mellow towards her. Sally was just so gentle, clean and quiet. She would be quiet when we visited anyone, lying down and relaxing almost immediately. No fuss, except maybe when a packet of food was rustled!

Greyhounds have short coats and shed few hairs. As Sally was mainly white, I thought that we would be bathing her a lot, but it was not the case. Somehow she managed to keep herself clean and a twice-yearly bath was all she ever needed, just to keep her smelling nice. We always bathed her outside on warm days. The bathroom was the one room that Sally never chose to enter. John and I feel sure that her previous owners must have put her in their bath. Even on holidays, Sally would avoid bathrooms. She didn't like the outdoor baths either, but was resigned to them and usually stood still for us to wash her. She didn't dislike water, though, and when walking on a warm day she would take the opportunity to have a paddle, even lying down in the shallows occasionally, in a river or lake. But try to have a play in the garden with a hose sprinkler: she hated it!

Sally wasn't a cuddly hound. Many greyhounds

do like cuddles and lots of attention, but Sally was always a bit aloof and independent. Sometimes I would sit beside her on the sofa, but she would rarely stay there for long. Belly rubs were a different matter; she would love to lie on her back and let us stroke her belly.

Sally often enjoyed a paddle if we came across a shallow river or lake, even lying down on a hot day.

Friends

Sally had many friends, human and canine, but there were four dogs in particular that we all shared special bonds with and great friendships were made.

Treacle, a black greyhound, and Lily, a lurcher, were both about the same age as Sally. Treacle was homed from the same kennels as Sally and therefore her owner took her along to the same local walks as us. Lily's owners heard about the walks and took Lily along to help her socialise with other dogs. Both hounds, like Sally, had very gentle natures and as they got to see each other at the walks, they came to know each other well and we humans always had plenty to talk about. As they were all seniors, we called them our 'Golden Girls'. We are all indebted to our hounds for bringing us together and allowing us such special friendships of the human and canine kind.

Sally, Lily and Treacle – the 'Golden Girls'

Treacle came for a visit to our house one day and Sally was totally nonplussed having her friend round. She just got onto the sofa and roached whilst Treacle played and was spinning round on the floor of the living room. Some greyhounds do this spinning act, where they almost pirouette on their back legs, turning in tight circles. Sally never did; her joints were probably not agile enough to cope. It is so funny to watch a greyhound spinning, and thankfully after frantically spinning one way, they usually have the sense to then spin in the other direction – otherwise they would end up very dizzy!

Sally and Treacle in our garden

Lily and Sally on a day out together

Sally met Winnie and Toby through her trips on the trains. Winnie, a black labrador, was typical of her breed and was always on the lookout for food. Her owners adored dogs and we soon got chatting and regularly met up on the preserved railways, often sharing a compartment. Both dogs had their blankets to put on the seats. We'd take turns to bring the chicken as treats for the dogs.

Sally and Winnie together on the trains

Toby was an elderly laid-back corgi/Jack Russell cross. He was a dignified kind of character, very gentle, and his owners were also dog lovers. Sally was very happy spending time with them and we all became good friends, even meeting up on holidays. Toby also knew Winnie, so occasionally we'd all get together for a day on the trains – room in the compartments could get quite tight!

Sally and Toby, asleep on a train ride and at a charity dog show together. It was Toby's first ever show and he won!

Final Days

As each year went by we knew how lucky we were that Sally kept so fit and well. When she got to 13, her legs weren't quite as good as they had been and she began to show mild symptoms of canine dementia. She would stand in the garden and just stare into space and be generally unsettled in the house, especially overnight. We had many sleepless nights as she paced about. With trial and error we found a pill that helped her, and along with mild painkillers to ease her joints, she was pretty much her usual self again. She still loved her walks and outings and we took the plunge and let her off lead on the beach. Armed with some tasty bits of sausage, John walked her away from me and she ran back to me for the treats. She loved it, but we were glad when she was safely back on the lead.

Sally off lead on the beach

37

We knew every moment with Sally now was so precious. Her zest for life continued, accompanying us everywhere like she'd always done, despite being diagnosed with a suspected slipped disc in her back. By leaving a webcam on her at home I realised she wasn't as happy being left alone any more so she occasionally came to work with me and lay in the corner of the office. She was so quiet that many of the staff didn't even realise she was there.

Just days before her 14th birthday we once again hired the horse arena with some friends. We expected Sally to just have a trot about, but she was obviously feeling good and had a great run round.

Sally at full stretch in the horse arena days before her 14th birthday
PHOTO CREDIT – Marcus Leeder

A few days later we held a birthday party for her. We invited her special hound friends and their owners to our favourite dog-friendly pub. We had a walk around the village as we'd done many times before over the last four and a half years. At the pub we were delighted to see they had put a message on the board outside. Never mind the weekly pub quiz or the next live music; it was

Sally's birthday and it was chalked on the board for all to see! We all had lunch in the beer garden, complete with sausages and birthday cake for the hounds. Sally was in her element and was the perfect hostess, walking round each person in turn to say hello. Of course, she was actually looking for treats, but it looked good and she got lots of cuddles and gifts from everyone.

Sally's birthday marked on the board at the pub!

A couple of weeks later we attended the monthly Greyhound Walk in the forest, but opted for a short amble round the lake as her legs and body were getting tired. It was the last time that Sally was with her friends and her last outing. It was heartbreaking to say goodbye to our very special girl. Sally not only touched our hearts, but clearly, by the tributes that came in, she had won the hearts of everyone who had met her. She was beautiful, independent, sometimes aloof, wise, gentle, and increasingly a cheeky girl. We always thought of her as a matriarch figure – strong and no nonsense!

Many people thought we had worked wonders with this 'unhomeable hound', and yes, we certainly had our tough times with her. She wasn't a straightforward hound, but without doubt, the best thing we've ever done in our lives was to give Sally a home.

Sally's legacy lives on and always will. She taught John and me all about greyhounds, their quirky habits, gentle nature and calm but cheeky temperaments. Thanks to Sally, we will always have greyhounds in our hearts – and hopefully in our home too.

'Saving one greyhound won't change the world, but for that one greyhound the world will change forever', was so fitting of Sally. By giving her a home, we gave her what she wanted most – love, comfort, regular walks and freedom from kennel life.

Sally enjoying her 14th birthday cake in the pub beer garden

Sky

After losing Sally we found that the first time of doing anything, like returning home to an empty house or eating our meal without her watching us, was so very hard and upsetting. A week without Sally passed by and John and I were out for a walk around town. It still felt very sad without Sally beside us. Our direct route home was via the playing field, a place we had visited regularly for walkies. I wanted to avoid it, but John encouraged me to go that way, knowing that the first time would be the worst and then it would be easier the next time. We entered the playing field and for the first time ever we saw a beautiful red kite fly straight over our heads. We had spent many years birdwatching before greyhounds came into our lives and red kites were one of our favourite birds, but at the time it was extremely rare, despite them being reintroduced and expanding their territories, for them to be seen near our town. We felt honoured and wondered if it was Sally connecting with us.

We had various short breaks and holidays that summer, but life seemed incomplete without Sally. We focused on moving house and as soon as our new home was ready (we made sure the garden fence was the first thing to be completed!), we began looking for a hound to join us. We went to the homing kennels and met a two-year-old black girl called Sky. She had only arrived from

41

the racing kennel a couple of days previously and had no interest in us – she was far more intrigued by the different smells around the paddock.

Two weeks later we took Sky to an organised greyhound walk. She walked around with us, didn't put a paw wrong, but there was no real connection between us. After having Sally choose us, it seemed that trying to pick a new hound was very hard to do. How did you know when it was the right dog for you? After the walk, we took Sky to our favourite pub, and as it was a nice day we sat in the beer garden for our lunch. Sky was suddenly in her element. Her cheeky nature came out and when our food arrived she was up on her back legs, front legs on the picnic bench. She loved chips! She even gave me 'kisses'. We decided that Sky was the one for us: she was going to be our new hound.

Sky giving me a kiss in the pub beer garden

Amazingly, as we finished our lunch, a red kite flew over the beer garden. They were quite a common sight there, but this particular bird flew very low, the lowest we'd ever seen. We took this as a sign from Sally. We'd chosen Sky and she approved!

We were sure we would have lots of fun ahead with Sky, but we will never ever forget our beautiful heart hound, Sally.

Sally aged 12, and Sky aged 2, both enjoying the garden

Made in the USA
Las Vegas, NV
22 April 2024